SATOSHI SCRIBE

Crypto Taxation Simplified:
Navigating the Complexities of
Cryptocurrency Taxes

Copyright © 2024 by Satoshi Scribe

All rights reserved. No part of this publication may be reproduced, stored or transmitted in any form or by any means, electronic, mechanical, photocopying, recording, scanning, or otherwise without written permission from the publisher. It is illegal to copy this book, post it to a website, or distribute it by any other means without permission.

First edition

*This book was professionally typeset on Reedsy.
Find out more at reedsy.com*

Contents

Why Understanding Crypto Taxes Matters	1
Foundational Concepts of Cryptocurrency Taxation	4
Detailed Filing Instructions	8
Strategies for Minimizing Tax Liability	13
International Considerations	17
Latest Legal and Regulatory Insights	22
Practical Tools and Resources	27
Legal Loopholes in Cryptocurrency Taxation	31
Illegal Loopholes and Their Consequences	35
Case Study: Maximizing Tax Efficiency with Legal Loopholes	39
Case Study 2: Strategic Use of Legal Loopholes for...	44
Case Study 3: The Dangers of Using Illegal Loopholes in...	50
Case Study: Comparing Tax Implications of Holding vs....	56
Tips for Building a Portfolio to Maximize Profits	62
No-Fuss Way to Track Crypto Taxes for the Lazy Trader	68
Conclusion: Simplifying Your Crypto Tax Journey	73

Why Understanding Crypto Taxes Matters

Welcome to the world of cryptocurrency taxation! If you're like most investors, the idea of dealing with taxes on your crypto transactions might seem daunting. But fear not—this chapter is here to guide you through the basics, helping you understand why it's crucial to get a handle on your tax obligations.

The Basics of Crypto Taxation

First things first: Why is cryptocurrency taxed? Simply put, governments view cryptocurrency as property, much like stocks or real estate. This means that whenever you buy, sell, trade, or earn crypto, you're potentially facing a taxable event.

Imagine you bought 1 Bitcoin (BTC) a year ago for $10,000, and today it's worth $15,000. If you decide to sell that Bitcoin now, you've made a $5,000 profit. This profit is what the tax authorities are interested in.

Why Should You Care?

Understanding and complying with crypto tax laws isn't just about avoiding penalties—it's about taking control of your financial future. Accurate tax reporting can:

- **Prevent Costly Penalties**: Non-compliance can lead to hefty fines and interest charges.
- **Enhance Your Financial Planning**: Knowing your tax obligations helps you make more informed investment decisions.
- **Increase Your Confidence**: With the right knowledge, you can navigate the tax season with ease, rather than dread.

A Real-World Example

Let's look at a real-world example. Jane is a cryptocurrency investor who started trading two years ago. In her first year, she didn't realize that her crypto trades needed to be reported. When tax season came around, she was confused and overwhelmed, leading to errors on her tax return.

Fast forward to this year—Jane has educated herself on the basics of crypto taxation. She keeps detailed records of her transactions, uses crypto tax software to track her gains and losses, and consults a tax advisor for complex issues. As a result, filing her taxes is now a straightforward process, saving her time, stress, and money.

Your Journey Starts Here

This book will take you through everything you need to know about cryptocurrency taxation, from foundational concepts to advanced strategies. By the end of this journey, you'll have the knowledge and tools to handle your crypto taxes confidently and efficiently.

So, let's dive in and start demystifying the world of crypto taxes together!

Foundational Concepts of Cryptocurrency Taxation

Understanding the foundational concepts of cryptocurrency taxation is essential for any investor. This chapter will break down the key elements you need to know, from taxable events to capital gains and cost basis. By the end of this chapter, you'll have a solid grasp of how cryptocurrency is taxed and be better prepared to manage your tax obligations.

Taxable Events in Cryptocurrency

A taxable event is any transaction or activity that triggers a tax liability. In the world of cryptocurrency, several common activities are considered taxable events:

1. **Selling Cryptocurrency for Fiat Currency**: Converting your cryptocurrency into traditional money (e.g., USD, EUR) is a taxable event. You must report any gain or loss based on the difference between the selling price and your cost basis.
2. **Trading One Cryptocurrency for Another**: When you trade Bitcoin for Ethereum, for example, it's considered a taxable

event. You must calculate the gain or loss based on the fair market value of the cryptocurrency at the time of the trade.
3. **Using Cryptocurrency to Purchase Goods or Services**: Spending cryptocurrency to buy goods or services is also a taxable event. The difference between the cost basis of the cryptocurrency and its fair market value at the time of purchase determines your gain or loss.
4. **Earning Cryptocurrency as Income**: If you receive cryptocurrency as payment for goods or services, as a reward for mining, or through staking, it's considered ordinary income. You must report this income at its fair market value at the time you received it.

Capital Gains vs. Ordinary Income

It's crucial to understand the difference between capital gains and ordinary income, as they are taxed differently:

- **Capital Gains**: These occur when you sell or trade cryptocurrency. If you sell your crypto at a higher price than what you paid for it, you have a capital gain. Conversely, if you sell it for less, you have a capital loss. Capital gains can be classified as short-term or long-term, depending on how long you've held the cryptocurrency.
- **Short-Term Gains**: If you hold the cryptocurrency for less than a year before selling it, any gain is considered short-term and taxed at your ordinary income tax rate.
- **Long-Term Gains**: If you hold the cryptocurrency for more than a year, the gain is considered long-term and typically taxed at a lower rate than short-term gains.
- **Ordinary Income**: Cryptocurrency received as payment for

services, mining rewards, or staking income is taxed as ordinary income. This means it is subject to the same tax rates as your salary or wages.

Cost Basis and Fair Market Value

Two critical concepts in calculating your tax liability are cost basis and fair market value (FMV):

- **Cost Basis**: This is the original value of the cryptocurrency when you acquired it. It includes the purchase price and any associated fees. For example, if you bought 1 Bitcoin for $10,000 and paid a $100 transaction fee, your cost basis would be $10,100.
- **Fair Market Value (FMV)**: This is the value of the cryptocurrency at the time of the transaction. For example, if you bought 1 Bitcoin for $10,000 and it is worth $15,000 when you sell it, the FMV at the time of sale is $15,000.

Holding Periods and Tax Rates

The length of time you hold your cryptocurrency before selling or trading it affects the tax rate applied to your gains:

- **Short-Term Gains**: If you hold your cryptocurrency for less than a year, any gains are taxed at your ordinary income tax rate, which can be as high as 37% in the United States.
- **Long-Term Gains**: If you hold your cryptocurrency for more than a year, you benefit from long-term capital gains tax rates, which are typically lower. In the United States, these rates are 0%, 15%, or 20%, depending on your income

level.

Example Scenario

Let's walk through an example to illustrate these concepts:

1. **Buying Cryptocurrency**: You purchase 2 Ethereum (ETH) at $1,000 each. Your total cost basis is $2,000.
2. **Holding Period**: You hold the ETH for 18 months.
3. **Selling Cryptocurrency**: You sell the 2 ETH for $3,000 each, resulting in total proceeds of $6,000.
4. **Calculating Gain**: Your capital gain is $6,000 (proceeds) - $2,000 (cost basis) = $4,000.
5. **Tax Rate**: Since you held the ETH for more than a year, the $4,000 gain is a long-term capital gain, taxed at a lower rate.

Summary

Understanding these foundational concepts is the first step toward mastering cryptocurrency taxation. By recognizing what constitutes a taxable event, distinguishing between capital gains and ordinary income, and calculating your cost basis and fair market value accurately, you'll be better prepared to handle your tax obligations. In the next chapter, we'll dive into the detailed steps of filing your cryptocurrency taxes, ensuring you can navigate the process with confidence.

Detailed Filing Instructions

Now that you understand the foundational concepts of cryptocurrency taxation, it's time to delve into the detailed steps of filing your taxes. This chapter will guide you through the process, ensuring you can accurately report your cryptocurrency transactions and comply with tax regulations. We'll cover the necessary forms and schedules, provide a step-by-step filing guide, and walk through some example scenarios to illustrate key points.

Reporting Crypto on Your Tax Return

To report your cryptocurrency transactions, you must follow a systematic approach:

1. **Identify Taxable Events**: Determine which of your transactions are taxable events.
2. **Calculate Gains and Losses**: For each taxable event, calculate the gain or loss based on your cost basis and the fair market value at the time of the transaction.
3. **Report on Tax Forms**: Use the appropriate tax forms to report these transactions to the tax authorities.

DETAILED FILING INSTRUCTIONS

Forms and Schedules Required

Here's a list of the primary forms and schedules you will need:

- **Form 8949**: Used to report sales and exchanges of capital assets, including cryptocurrency.
- **Schedule D**: Summarizes your total capital gains and losses.
- **Schedule 1**: Reports additional income such as earnings from mining or staking.
- **Form 1040**: The main income tax return form used by individual taxpayers in the United States.

Step-by-Step Filing Guide

Step 1: Gather Your Records

Collect detailed records of all your cryptocurrency transactions, including:

- Purchase and sale dates
- Purchase and sale prices
- Transaction fees
- Amounts of cryptocurrency involved
- Fair market value at the time of each transaction

Step 2: Calculate Gains and Losses

For each taxable event, calculate the gain or loss using the formula:

$$\text{Gain/Loss} = \text{Proceeds} - \text{Cost Basis}$$

- **Proceeds**: The amount you received from selling or trading

the cryptocurrency.
- **Cost Basis**: The original value of the cryptocurrency, including any fees.

Step 3: Fill Out Form 8949

Use Form 8949 to report each cryptocurrency transaction. You'll need to provide:

- Description of the property (e.g., 1 BTC)
- Date acquired
- Date sold or disposed of
- Proceeds
- Cost basis
- Gain or loss

Here's an example:

DescriptionDate AcquiredDate SoldProceedsCost Basis-Gain/Loss

1 BTC

01/01/2022

01/01/2023

$15,000

$10,100

$4,900

Step 4: Transfer Totals to Schedule D

Once you've completed Form 8949, transfer the totals to Schedule D. This form summarizes your capital gains and losses.

Step 5: Include Additional Income on Schedule 1

Report any cryptocurrency income earned from activities like mining or staking on Schedule 1. This income is treated as ordinary income and taxed at your regular income tax rate.

Step 6: Complete Form 1040

Include your summarized capital gains and losses from Schedule D and any additional income from Schedule 1 on your main tax return, Form 1040.

Example Scenarios

Example 1: Selling Cryptocurrency for Fiat

- **Transaction**: You bought 2 ETH for $1,000 each and sold them for $3,000 each.
- **Cost Basis**: $2,000 ($1,000 per ETH x 2)
- **Proceeds**: $6,000 ($3,000 per ETH x 2)
- **Gain**: $4,000 ($6,000 - $2,000)

Report this on Form 8949, transfer the total to Schedule D, and include it on Form 1040.

Example 2: Trading One Cryptocurrency for Another

- **Transaction**: You traded 1 BTC (bought for $10,000) for 10 ETH (worth $15,000 at the time of trade).
- **Cost Basis**: $10,000
- **Proceeds**: $15,000
- **Gain**: $5,000 ($15,000 - $10,000)

Report this on Form 8949, transfer the total to Schedule D, and include it on Form 1040.

Example 3: Earning Cryptocurrency as Income

- **Transaction**: You mined 0.5 BTC, which was worth $10,000 at the time of mining.

- **Ordinary Income**: $10,000

Report this income on Schedule 1 and include it on Form 1040.

Common Mistakes to Avoid

1. **Ignoring Small Transactions**: Even small transactions can add up and should be reported.
2. **Incorrect Cost Basis**: Ensure you accurately calculate the cost basis, including transaction fees.
3. **Missing Deadlines**: File your taxes on time to avoid penalties and interest.
4. **Not Keeping Records**: Maintain detailed records of all transactions for accurate reporting and potential audits.

Summary

Filing your cryptocurrency taxes may seem complex, but following a systematic approach can make the process manageable. By gathering detailed records, calculating gains and losses accurately, and using the correct forms, you can ensure compliance and avoid potential penalties. In the next chapter, we'll explore strategies for minimizing your tax liability, helping you optimize your tax position and potentially save money.

Strategies for Minimizing Tax Liability

Minimizing your tax liability is a crucial aspect of managing your cryptocurrency investments. By strategically planning your transactions and understanding the tax implications, you can reduce the amount of tax you owe. This chapter will explore various strategies to help you optimize your tax situation, including long-term vs. short-term gains, tax-loss harvesting, crypto donations, and utilizing tax-advantaged accounts.

Long-Term vs. Short-Term Gains

One of the simplest strategies to minimize your tax liability is to hold your cryptocurrency for more than a year before selling. This can significantly reduce the tax rate on your gains.

- **Short-Term Gains**: If you sell cryptocurrency that you've held for less than a year, the gain is considered short-term and is taxed at your ordinary income tax rate. This rate can be as high as 37% in the United States.
- **Long-Term Gains**: If you hold your cryptocurrency for more than a year before selling, the gain is considered long-term and is taxed at a lower rate. In the United States, long-

term capital gains tax rates are 0%, 15%, or 20%, depending on your income level.

Example Scenario

You bought 1 Bitcoin (BTC) for $10,000. If you sell it after six months for $15,000, the $5,000 gain is a short-term gain and will be taxed at your ordinary income tax rate. However, if you sell it after 18 months for $15,000, the $5,000 gain is a long-term gain and will be taxed at the lower long-term capital gains rate.

Tax-Loss Harvesting

Tax-loss harvesting involves selling cryptocurrency at a loss to offset gains from other investments. This strategy can reduce your overall tax liability.

- **Offsetting Gains**: You can use losses from cryptocurrency sales to offset gains from other investments, such as stocks. This can lower your taxable income.
- **Carrying Over Losses**: If your losses exceed your gains, you can carry over the excess loss to future tax years, up to a certain limit.

Example Scenario

You have a $10,000 gain from selling some Ethereum (ETH). You also have a $4,000 loss from selling Bitcoin (BTC). You can use the $4,000 loss to offset the $10,000 gain, reducing your taxable gain to $6,000.

Crypto Donations

Donating cryptocurrency to a qualified charity can provide a tax deduction based on the fair market value of the cryptocurrency at the time of donation. This strategy not only helps reduce your tax liability but also supports charitable causes.

- **Tax Deduction**: When you donate cryptocurrency, you can deduct the fair market value of the donation from your taxable income, provided you have held the cryptocurrency for more than a year.
- **Avoiding Capital Gains Tax**: Donating cryptocurrency allows you to avoid paying capital gains tax on the appreciated value of the cryptocurrency.

Example Scenario
You bought 1 Bitcoin (BTC) for $5,000 and it is now worth $20,000. If you donate the Bitcoin to a qualified charity, you can claim a $20,000 tax deduction and avoid paying capital gains tax on the $15,000 appreciation.

Utilizing Tax-Advantaged Accounts

Investing in cryptocurrency through tax-advantaged accounts, such as a self-directed Individual Retirement Account (IRA), can help defer or eliminate taxes on your gains.

- **Self-Directed IRA**: A self-directed IRA allows you to hold a variety of investments, including cryptocurrency. Gains within the IRA are not taxed until you withdraw the funds.
- **Roth IRA**: With a Roth IRA, contributions are made with

after-tax dollars, but qualified withdrawals, including gains, are tax-free. This can be particularly advantageous if you expect your investments to grow significantly.

Example Scenario

You invest $10,000 in Bitcoin (BTC) through a self-directed Roth IRA. Over several years, the value of your Bitcoin grows to $50,000. When you withdraw the funds in retirement, the $40,000 gain is tax-free.

Summary

By strategically managing your cryptocurrency investments, you can minimize your tax liability and maximize your after-tax returns. Holding your cryptocurrency for the long term, utilizing tax-loss harvesting, making charitable donations, and investing through tax-advantaged accounts are all effective strategies. In the next chapter, we'll explore international considerations for cryptocurrency taxation, including cross-border transactions and reporting requirements in different countries.

International Considerations

Cryptocurrency investors often engage in transactions across borders, making it essential to understand the tax implications in different jurisdictions. This chapter will cover the complexities of international cryptocurrency taxation, including cross-border transactions, reporting requirements in various countries, double taxation agreements, and case studies of international tax compliance.

Tax Implications for Cross-Border Transactions

When you engage in cryptocurrency transactions that cross national borders, you may be subject to tax laws in multiple countries. Here are some key considerations:

- **Residency and Taxation**: Your tax obligations generally depend on your residency status. Most countries tax their residents on worldwide income, meaning you must report and pay taxes on all your cryptocurrency transactions, regardless of where they occur.
- **Source of Income**: Some countries tax income based on its source. If you earn cryptocurrency income from activities conducted within a particular country, you may need to pay

taxes there.

Example Scenario

You are a US resident who trades on a European exchange and earns staking rewards from a Singapore-based blockchain project. You must report all these transactions on your US tax return, as the US taxes residents on worldwide income. Additionally, you may have reporting obligations in Europe and Singapore, depending on their tax laws.

Reporting Requirements in Different Countries

Each country has its own rules and regulations regarding cryptocurrency taxation. Here are some examples of reporting requirements in major jurisdictions:

- **United States**: The IRS requires taxpayers to report cryptocurrency transactions on Form 8949 and Schedule D. Income from mining or staking must be reported on Schedule 1. Additionally, you must answer "Yes" to the virtual currency question on Form 1040 if you engaged in any cryptocurrency transactions during the tax year.
- **United Kingdom**: HMRC treats cryptocurrency as property. You must report capital gains on the Self Assessment tax return and pay Capital Gains Tax (CGT) on profits. Income from mining or staking is treated as taxable income and must be reported accordingly.
- **Canada**: The Canada Revenue Agency (CRA) considers cryptocurrency to be a commodity. Cryptocurrency transactions are subject to capital gains tax or business income tax, depending on the nature of the transactions. Gains and

losses must be reported on your income tax return.
- **Australia**: The Australian Taxation Office (ATO) requires taxpayers to report cryptocurrency transactions as capital gains. If you are carrying on a business of trading or mining cryptocurrency, it is treated as ordinary income. Transactions must be reported on your tax return, and detailed records must be kept.

Double Taxation Agreements

Double taxation agreements (DTAs) are treaties between two countries designed to prevent the same income from being taxed twice. These agreements typically allow for tax credits or exemptions to mitigate the impact of double taxation.

- **Tax Credits**: If you pay tax on cryptocurrency income in one country, you may be eligible for a tax credit in your home country, reducing your overall tax liability.
- **Exemptions**: Some DTAs provide for exemptions where only one country has the right to tax specific types of income.

Example Scenario

You are a resident of the United Kingdom who earns staking rewards from a blockchain project based in Germany. Under the DTA between the UK and Germany, you may be able to claim a tax credit for the German tax paid on your staking rewards, reducing your UK tax liability.

Case Studies of International Tax Compliance

Case Study 1: United States and United Kingdom

John is a US resident who holds and trades cryptocurrency on a UK-based exchange. He earns staking rewards and sells some of his holdings for a profit. John must report all his transactions on his US tax return. Because he traded on a UK exchange and earned staking rewards, he may also have UK tax obligations. John consults a tax advisor to ensure compliance with both US and UK tax laws and utilizes the US-UK DTA to avoid double taxation.

Case Study 2: Germany

Anna is a resident of Germany who has been holding Bitcoin for three years. She decides to sell her Bitcoin and realizes a significant gain. In Germany, cryptocurrency held for more than one year is exempt from capital gains tax. Therefore, Anna does not have to pay tax on the sale of her Bitcoin, making Germany a favorable jurisdiction for long-term holders.

Case Study 3: Canada and Australia

Lisa is a Canadian resident who works remotely for an Australian company and is paid in cryptocurrency. She must report this income on her Canadian tax return as ordinary income. Due to the DTA between Canada and Australia, Lisa can claim a foreign tax credit for any Australian tax withheld, reducing her Canadian tax liability.

Summary

Navigating the complexities of international cryptocurrency taxation requires a thorough understanding of the tax laws in each relevant jurisdiction. By recognizing the tax implications of cross-border transactions, complying with reporting requirements, and leveraging double taxation agreements, you can manage your tax obligations more effectively. In the next chapter, we will explore the latest legal and regulatory insights, helping you stay informed about recent changes and future trends in cryptocurrency taxation.

Latest Legal and Regulatory Insights

Cryptocurrency taxation is an evolving field, with laws and regulations continually adapting to the rapid growth of digital assets. Staying informed about the latest legal and regulatory changes is crucial for ensuring compliance and optimizing your tax strategy. In this chapter, we will explore recent changes in crypto tax laws, the roles of key regulatory bodies, significant legal developments, and the importance of compliance to avoid penalties.

Recent Changes in Crypto Tax Laws

Recent years have seen significant changes in cryptocurrency tax laws as governments strive to regulate the growing market. Here are some notable updates:

- **IRS Updates in the United States**: The IRS has issued new guidance, including Revenue Ruling 2019-24, which addresses the tax treatment of hard forks and airdrops. The ruling clarifies that taxpayers must recognize income upon receipt of new cryptocurrency from a hard fork or airdrop.
- **UK's Cryptoasset Manual**: HMRC has published a comprehensive Cryptoasset Manual, detailing the tax treatment

of various cryptocurrency transactions, including trading, mining, and staking. This manual serves as a valuable resource for UK taxpayers.
- **EU's Fifth Anti-Money Laundering Directive (5AMLD)**: The European Union's 5AMLD requires cryptocurrency exchanges and wallet providers to implement KYC (Know Your Customer) and AML (Anti-Money Laundering) procedures. This directive aims to enhance transparency and reduce illicit activities in the crypto space.
- **Australia's Updated Guidance**: The ATO has updated its guidance on the tax treatment of cryptocurrency, emphasizing the need for accurate record-keeping and clear reporting of capital gains and income from crypto activities.

Key Regulatory Bodies and Their Roles

Several regulatory bodies play crucial roles in overseeing cryptocurrency taxation and compliance. Understanding their functions can help you navigate the regulatory landscape more effectively:

- **Internal Revenue Service (IRS) – United States**: The IRS is responsible for enforcing tax laws in the United States. It provides guidance on the tax treatment of cryptocurrency and ensures compliance through audits and penalties for non-compliance.
- **HM Revenue & Customs (HMRC) – United Kingdom**: HMRC oversees tax collection and enforcement in the UK. It provides detailed guidance on cryptocurrency taxation and requires taxpayers to report their crypto transactions accurately.

- **Australian Taxation Office (ATO) – Australia**: The ATO administers tax laws in Australia, including those related to cryptocurrency. It offers guidance and resources to help taxpayers comply with their crypto tax obligations.
- **European Union (EU)**: The EU sets regulatory standards for member states, including anti-money laundering directives and tax reporting requirements for cryptocurrency transactions.

Legal Developments and Future Trends

The legal landscape for cryptocurrency taxation is continuously evolving. Here are some key developments and future trends to watch:

- **Increased Regulatory Scrutiny**: Governments worldwide are increasing their scrutiny of cryptocurrency transactions to combat tax evasion and illicit activities. Expect more stringent reporting requirements and audits.
- **Blockchain Analytics**: Tax authorities are leveraging blockchain analytics tools to track cryptocurrency transactions and identify non-compliance. This technology enhances their ability to detect unreported income and gains.
- **Global Tax Cooperation**: Countries are collaborating on tax enforcement, sharing information to ensure taxpayers comply with international tax laws. This trend is likely to continue, leading to more comprehensive and coordinated tax regulations.
- **Regulation of Decentralized Finance (DeFi)**: As DeFi platforms grow in popularity, regulators are seeking ways to

oversee and tax these transactions. Future regulations may address the unique challenges posed by DeFi activities.

Compliance and Penalties for Non-Compliance

Compliance with cryptocurrency tax laws is essential to avoid penalties and legal issues. Here are some common compliance requirements and potential penalties for non-compliance:

- **Accurate Reporting**: Ensure that you report all taxable cryptocurrency transactions accurately on your tax return. Failure to do so can result in penalties and interest on unpaid taxes.
- **Record-Keeping**: Maintain detailed records of all your cryptocurrency transactions, including dates, amounts, and purposes. Inadequate record-keeping can lead to errors in reporting and potential audits.
- **Timely Filing**: File your tax returns on time to avoid late filing penalties. If you owe taxes, ensure timely payment to avoid interest and late payment penalties.
- **Penalties for Non-Compliance**: Penalties for failing to report cryptocurrency transactions can be severe. In the United States, for example, penalties can include fines of up to $250,000 and imprisonment for up to five years for willful failure to file a tax return.

Summary

Staying informed about the latest legal and regulatory changes is crucial for navigating the complexities of cryptocurrency taxation. By understanding recent updates, recognizing the roles of key regulatory bodies, and complying with tax laws, you can optimize your tax strategy and avoid penalties. In the next chapter, we will explore practical tools and resources to help streamline your tax reporting process, ensuring a smooth and efficient experience.

Practical Tools and Resources

Managing your cryptocurrency tax obligations can be challenging, but there are numerous tools and resources available to help streamline the process. This chapter will explore cryptocurrency tax software, useful websites and online tools, professional services, and best practices for record-keeping. These resources will make it easier for you to accurately report your cryptocurrency transactions and stay compliant with tax regulations.

Cryptocurrency Tax Software

Cryptocurrency tax software can simplify the process of calculating gains and losses, generating tax reports, and ensuring accurate filings. Here are some popular options:

- **CoinTracking**: CoinTracking is a comprehensive tool that tracks your cryptocurrency transactions, calculates gains and losses, and generates detailed tax reports. It supports over 10,000 cryptocurrencies and integrates with multiple exchanges and wallets.
- **CryptoTrader.Tax**: This user-friendly platform allows you to import your transaction history, calculate gains and

losses, and generate tax reports in minutes. It supports integration with popular exchanges and provides step-by-step guidance for filing your taxes.
- **TokenTax**: TokenTax offers a range of services, from basic tax reporting to full-service tax preparation. It supports all major exchanges and provides detailed reports for both capital gains and income from cryptocurrency activities.
- **Koinly**: Koinly helps you calculate your cryptocurrency taxes, generate tax reports, and track your portfolio. It supports integration with over 300 exchanges and wallets and offers country-specific tax reports.

Useful Websites and Online Tools

Several websites and online tools can provide valuable information and assistance with cryptocurrency taxation:

- **IRS Virtual Currency Tax Center**: The IRS provides resources and guidance on the tax treatment of virtual currencies, including FAQs and updates on recent developments. Visit the IRS Virtual Currency Tax Center for more information.
- **HMRC Cryptoassets Manual**: HMRC offers a detailed manual on the tax treatment of cryptoassets, covering topics such as capital gains, income tax, and record-keeping. Access the manual here.
- **CoinMarketCap**: CoinMarketCap provides historical price data for thousands of cryptocurrencies, which can be useful for calculating fair market value and cost basis. Visit CoinMarketCap for more information.
- **CryptoCompare**: CryptoCompare offers tools for tracking

cryptocurrency prices, portfolios, and market data. It also provides a tax calculator to help you estimate your tax liability. Visit CryptoCompare for more information.

Professional Services: Accountants and Tax Advisors

Consulting with a tax professional who specializes in cryptocurrency can provide valuable insights and ensure accurate tax reporting. Here are some tips for finding the right professional:

- **Look for Experience**: Choose a tax professional with experience in cryptocurrency taxation. They should be familiar with the unique challenges and opportunities associated with crypto investments.
- **Verify Credentials**: Ensure that the tax professional is certified and in good standing with relevant professional organizations, such as the American Institute of Certified Public Accountants (AICPA) or the Chartered Institute of Taxation (CIOT).
- **Ask for References**: Request references from other cryptocurrency investors who have worked with the tax professional. This can provide insights into their expertise and reliability.

Record-Keeping Tips and Best Practices

Maintaining detailed records of your cryptocurrency transactions is essential for accurate tax reporting and compliance. Here are some best practices for record-keeping:

- **Track All Transactions**: Keep a detailed record of every

cryptocurrency transaction, including purchases, sales, trades, and income from mining or staking. Include dates, amounts, and transaction IDs.
- **Use Multiple Backups**: Store your records in multiple locations, such as cloud storage, external hard drives, and physical copies. This ensures that you have access to your records in case of data loss.
- **Organize by Category**: Organize your records by category, such as capital gains, income, and expenses. This makes it easier to calculate gains and losses and prepare your tax return.
- **Regularly Update Records**: Update your records regularly to ensure they are current and accurate. This can help you avoid last-minute stress during tax season.

Summary

Utilizing practical tools and resources can significantly simplify the process of managing your cryptocurrency taxes. Cryptocurrency tax software, useful websites, professional services, and diligent record-keeping practices can help you accurately report your transactions and stay compliant with tax regulations. In the next chapter, we will provide a comprehensive conclusion, recapping the key points and offering final tips for a smooth tax reporting process.

Legal Loopholes in Cryptocurrency Taxation

Navigating the complexities of cryptocurrency taxation can often reveal legal loopholes that savvy investors can use to minimize their tax liabilities. This chapter will explore several legal strategies and opportunities that exist within the framework of current tax laws, allowing you to optimize your tax outcomes while remaining fully compliant with regulations.

Understanding Legal Loopholes

A legal loophole is an opportunity within the law that allows you to reduce your tax liability without violating any legal requirements. These strategies exploit ambiguities or specific provisions in the tax code to your advantage.

Common Legal Loopholes

1. **Tax-Loss Harvesting**

Tax-loss harvesting involves selling underperforming assets at a loss to offset gains from other investments. This strategy can significantly reduce your taxable income:

- **How It Works**: If you have made significant gains on some cryptocurrency investments, you can sell other holdings that are currently at a loss. The losses can offset your gains, thereby reducing your overall tax liability.
- **Example**: You made $10,000 in gains from Bitcoin but have $5,000 in losses from Ethereum. Selling the Ethereum at a loss can reduce your taxable gain to $5,000.

2. Long-Term vs. Short-Term Capital Gains

Understanding the difference between long-term and short-term capital gains can help you plan your trades to minimize taxes:

- **Short-Term Capital Gains**: These apply to assets held for less than a year and are taxed at your ordinary income tax rate.
- **Long-Term Capital Gains**: These apply to assets held for more than a year and are taxed at a lower rate (0%, 15%, or 20%, depending on your income level).
- **Strategy**: By holding your cryptocurrencies for longer than a year before selling, you can benefit from lower tax rates on your gains.

3. Like-Kind Exchanges (1031 Exchanges)

While traditionally used for real estate, some investors have explored the use of 1031 exchanges for cryptocurrency. However, this strategy is highly contentious and its applicability to cryptocurrencies has been limited since the 2018 tax law changes:

- **How It Works**: A like-kind exchange allows you to defer capital gains taxes by reinvesting the proceeds from the sale

of an asset into a similar asset.
- **Current Status**: The IRS has clarified that 1031 exchanges are no longer applicable to cryptocurrencies. Investors should be cautious and seek professional advice before attempting this strategy.

4. Gifting Cryptocurrency

Gifting cryptocurrency can be a tax-efficient way to transfer wealth without incurring significant tax liabilities:

- **Gift Tax Exclusion**: You can gift up to a certain amount ($15,000 per recipient in 2023) without incurring any gift tax.
- **How It Helps**: If you have significant cryptocurrency holdings, gifting some of them can reduce your taxable estate while also potentially benefiting the recipient with a lower tax bracket.

5. Charitable Donations

Donating cryptocurrency to a qualified charitable organization can provide a dual tax benefit:

- **Deduction**: You can deduct the fair market value of the donated cryptocurrency on your tax return.
- **Avoid Capital Gains**: By donating appreciated assets, you avoid paying capital gains taxes on the increase in value.

Best Practices for Using Legal Loopholes

To ensure you are utilizing these strategies effectively and legally:

- **Consult a Tax Professional**: Always seek advice from a qualified tax professional who understands cryptocurrency taxation.
- **Keep Detailed Records**: Maintain comprehensive records of all transactions, including purchase and sale dates, amounts, and transaction IDs.
- **Stay Informed**: Tax laws and regulations regarding cryptocurrencies are constantly evolving. Keep up-to-date with the latest guidance from tax authorities.

Summary

Leveraging legal loopholes in cryptocurrency taxation can help you minimize your tax liability while staying compliant with the law. Strategies like tax-loss harvesting, understanding capital gains classifications, gifting, and charitable donations offer legitimate ways to optimize your tax outcomes. Always consult with a tax professional and keep detailed records to ensure compliance and maximize your benefits.

Illegal Loopholes and Their Consequences

While there are legal ways to minimize your cryptocurrency tax liability, it's crucial to understand the boundaries between legal tax strategies and illegal tax evasion. This chapter will examine illegal loopholes, the consequences of engaging in them, and the importance of staying compliant with tax regulations.

Understanding Illegal Loopholes

Illegal loopholes involve actions that are explicitly against the law, designed to evade taxes and deceive tax authorities. These actions can lead to severe legal consequences, including fines, penalties, and imprisonment.

Common Illegal Loopholes

1. **Failing to Report Cryptocurrency Transactions**
One of the most common forms of tax evasion is simply not reporting cryptocurrency transactions:

- **How It Works**: Some investors may believe that because

cryptocurrencies are decentralized and transactions are pseudonymous, they can avoid reporting them on their tax returns.
- **Consequences**: The IRS and other tax authorities are increasingly using sophisticated tools to track cryptocurrency transactions. Failing to report can result in significant penalties and interest, and in severe cases, criminal charges.

2. Using Offshore Accounts to Hide Assets

Some individuals attempt to hide their cryptocurrency holdings in offshore accounts to avoid taxation:

- **How It Works**: By transferring cryptocurrency to an account in a country with lenient tax laws, individuals hope to keep their assets out of reach of domestic tax authorities.
- **Consequences**: The IRS has stringent regulations and penalties for failing to report foreign accounts. The Foreign Account Tax Compliance Act (FATCA) requires U.S. taxpayers to report foreign financial assets, and non-compliance can lead to severe penalties and criminal prosecution.

3. False Reporting of Transactions

Deliberately misreporting transactions to minimize tax liability is another illegal practice:

- **How It Works**: This can involve inflating the cost basis to reduce taxable gains, or falsely claiming losses.
- **Consequences**: Submitting false information on tax returns is a serious offense. If discovered, it can lead to audits, fines, penalties, and potential criminal charges.

4. Using Anonymity to Evade Taxes

Relying on the anonymity provided by certain cryptocurrencies to evade taxes is illegal:

- **How It Works**: Investors may use privacy coins or decentralized exchanges that do not require identity verification to hide their transactions from tax authorities.
- **Consequences**: Tax authorities are increasingly able to trace transactions involving privacy coins. Engaging in such practices can result in significant legal repercussions.

The Consequences of Illegal Loopholes

Engaging in illegal tax evasion strategies can lead to severe consequences, including:

- **Fines and Penalties**: The IRS imposes heavy fines and penalties on those who fail to report cryptocurrency transactions or provide false information. Penalties can include a percentage of the unpaid tax, interest on the unpaid amount, and additional fines.
- **Audits**: If you are suspected of tax evasion, the IRS can conduct an audit, requiring you to provide detailed records of all your transactions. This can be a time-consuming and stressful process.
- **Criminal Charges**: In cases of willful tax evasion, the IRS can pursue criminal charges, which can result in imprisonment.
- **Damage to Reputation**: Being caught evading taxes can damage your personal and professional reputation, leading to long-term consequences beyond legal penalties.

The Importance of Compliance

Staying compliant with tax regulations is not only a legal obligation but also a way to ensure peace of mind and avoid the severe consequences associated with illegal tax evasion. Here are some tips to ensure compliance:

- **Report All Transactions**: Accurately report all your cryptocurrency transactions, including trades, sales, income, and gifts.
- **Keep Detailed Records**: Maintain comprehensive records of all transactions, including dates, amounts, and transaction IDs.
- **Consult a Professional**: Seek advice from a tax professional who understands cryptocurrency taxation to ensure you are following the law.
- **Stay Informed**: Keep up-to-date with changes in tax laws and regulations to ensure ongoing compliance.

Summary

While it may be tempting to use illegal loopholes to evade cryptocurrency taxes, the risks far outweigh the potential benefits. Engaging in illegal tax evasion practices can lead to severe legal consequences, including fines, penalties, audits, criminal charges, and damage to your reputation. It is essential to stay compliant with tax regulations, report all transactions accurately, and seek professional advice to navigate the complexities of cryptocurrency taxation legally and ethically.

Case Study: Maximizing Tax Efficiency with Legal Loopholes

Background

Sarah is a 35-year-old software engineer and avid cryptocurrency investor. She began investing in cryptocurrencies in 2017 and has built a diverse portfolio, including Bitcoin, Ethereum, and various altcoins. By 2023, her portfolio had grown significantly, and she faced a substantial tax liability. Sarah decided to consult a tax professional to explore legal strategies to minimize her tax burden.

Situation Analysis

In 2023, Sarah's portfolio saw the following changes:

- **Bitcoin**: Purchased 2 BTC in 2017 for $3,000 each. Sold 1 BTC in 2023 for $60,000.
- **Ethereum**: Purchased 10 ETH in 2018 for $500 each. Sold 5 ETH in 2023 for $4,000 each.
- **Altcoins**: Various small investments, some profitable, others at a loss.

Sarah's primary goal was to reduce her taxable gains legally while staying compliant with IRS regulations.

Strategies Implemented

Sarah's tax professional suggested several legal strategies to optimize her tax outcomes:

1. **Tax-Loss Harvesting**
2. **Long-Term Capital Gains**
3. **Charitable Donations**
4. **Gifting Cryptocurrency**

Strategy 1: Tax-Loss Harvesting

Implementation: Sarah's portfolio included several altcoins that were underperforming. She had invested $5,000 in an altcoin that had since dropped to $1,000.
Action:

- Sold the altcoin at a $4,000 loss.
- Used this loss to offset the capital gains from her Bitcoin sale.

Result:

- Capital gain from Bitcoin: $60,000 (sale) - $3,000 (cost basis) = $57,000
- Offset from altcoin loss: $57,000 - $4,000 = $53,000 taxable gain

Strategy 2: Long-Term Capital Gains

Implementation: Sarah held her Bitcoin and Ethereum for more than a year, qualifying her for long-term capital gains tax rates.
Action:

- Sold 1 BTC after holding it for over five years.
- Sold 5 ETH after holding them for more than four years.

Result:

- Long-term capital gains rates applied, which are lower than short-term rates.
- Assuming a 15% tax rate for long-term gains, Sarah's tax liability was significantly reduced compared to short-term rates, which could be as high as 37%.

Strategy 3: Charitable Donations

Implementation: Sarah wanted to support a charitable cause while benefiting from tax deductions.
Action:

- Donated 2 ETH to a qualified charity.
- Fair market value of the donation was $8,000 (2 ETH at $4,000 each).

Result:

- Sarah could deduct the fair market value of the donated cryptocurrency on her tax return, reducing her taxable income by $8,000.
- Avoided paying capital gains tax on the appreciated value of the donated ETH.

Strategy 4: Gifting Cryptocurrency

Implementation: Sarah had a niece who was interested in starting her own cryptocurrency investments. She decided to gift her niece some cryptocurrency.
Action:

- Gifted 0.5 BTC to her niece.
- Fair market value of the gift was $30,000.

Result:

- The gift fell under the annual gift tax exclusion limit ($15,000 per recipient for 2023).
- Sarah and her husband used their combined gift tax exclusion to cover the $30,000 gift without incurring any gift tax.
- The niece received the Bitcoin with a cost basis of $1,500 (proportional share of the original purchase price), which could benefit her when she decides to sell in the future.

Overall Impact

By strategically implementing these legal loopholes, Sarah significantly reduced her taxable income and optimized her tax outcomes. Here's a summary of her tax savings:

- **Taxable Gain from Bitcoin**: Reduced to $53,000 through tax-loss harvesting.
- **Tax Savings from Long-Term Gains**: Long-term capital gains tax rate of 15% applied to $53,000, resulting in $7,950 in taxes, compared to a potential $19,610 if short-term rates

had applied.
- **Charitable Donation**: $8,000 deduction reduced Sarah's taxable income.
- **Gift Exclusion**: Avoided gift tax on $30,000 by utilizing the combined gift tax exclusion limit.

Sarah's proactive approach and use of legal loopholes not only minimized her tax liability but also allowed her to support charitable causes and help her niece start her investment journey.

Conclusion

Sarah's case illustrates how a well-informed investor can leverage legal strategies to manage their cryptocurrency tax liabilities effectively. By understanding and applying tax-loss harvesting, long-term capital gains, charitable donations, and gifting, Sarah optimized her tax outcomes while remaining fully compliant with IRS regulations. This approach not only provided immediate tax benefits but also set up long-term advantages for her and her family.

Case Study 2: Strategic Use of Legal Loopholes for Optimizing Cryptocurrency Taxation

Background

Michael is a 40-year-old entrepreneur who has been investing in cryptocurrencies since 2016. His diverse portfolio includes Bitcoin, Ethereum, various DeFi tokens, and stablecoins. By 2023, Michael's portfolio had grown substantially, and he sought ways to minimize his tax liability using different legal strategies while ensuring compliance with tax regulations.

Situation Analysis

In 2023, Michael's portfolio saw the following changes:

- **Bitcoin**: Purchased 5 BTC in 2016 for $600 each. Sold 2 BTC in 2023 for $50,000 each.
- **Ethereum**: Purchased 50 ETH in 2017 for $300 each. Sold 25 ETH in 2023 for $3,500 each.
- **DeFi Tokens**: Various investments, some with significant gains, others with minor losses.
- **Stablecoins**: Held USDC and DAI for liquidity purposes.

Michael's goal was to explore various legal strategies to reduce his tax liability, optimize his gains, and ensure compliance with tax regulations.

Strategies Implemented

Michael's tax advisor suggested several strategies different from those used in the previous case study, including:

1. **Utilizing Tax-Advantaged Accounts**
2. **Making Use of Specific Identification Method**
3. **Crypto Loans and Collateral**
4. **Income Deferral through Timing Sales**

Strategy 1: Utilizing Tax-Advantaged Accounts

Implementation: Michael set up a self-directed Roth IRA to hold some of his cryptocurrency investments.

Action:

- Transferred a portion of his cryptocurrency investments into the Roth IRA.
- Continued to trade within the IRA, deferring taxes on gains.

Result:

- **Tax Benefits**: All gains within the Roth IRA are tax-free if withdrawals are made after the age of 59½ and the account has been open for at least five years.
- **Optimized Gains**: Allowed Michael to grow his investments without immediate tax consequences.

Strategy 2: Making Use of Specific Identification Method

Implementation: Michael had multiple purchases of Bitcoin and Ethereum over the years at different prices. He used the specific identification method to choose which units to sell, optimizing for tax benefits.

Action:

- For the Bitcoin sale, Michael chose to sell units with the highest cost basis first.
- For the Ethereum sale, he selected the units with the lowest cost basis, taking advantage of the long-term gains.

Result:

- **Minimized Taxable Gains**: Selling high-cost-basis Bitcoin reduced his capital gains.
- **Optimized Long-Term Gains**: Selling low-cost-basis Ethereum allowed him to benefit from the lower long-term capital gains tax rate.

Strategy 3: Crypto Loans and Collateral

Implementation: Michael utilized decentralized finance (DeFi) platforms to take out loans using his cryptocurrency as collateral instead of selling his assets.

Action:

- Borrowed stablecoins using his Bitcoin and Ethereum holdings as collateral.
- Used the stablecoins to invest in other opportunities and

manage liquidity.

Result:

- **Tax Deferral**: By taking out loans instead of selling his assets, Michael deferred realizing capital gains.
- **Maintained Portfolio Exposure**: Kept his Bitcoin and Ethereum positions intact, allowing them to potentially appreciate further.

Strategy 4: Income Deferral through Timing Sales

Implementation: Michael planned the timing of his sales to defer income to a future tax year when he expected to be in a lower tax bracket.
  Action:

- Sold 2 BTC and 25 ETH towards the end of the year but deferred additional sales to the following year.
- Spread sales across tax years to manage taxable income levels.

Result:

- **Tax Rate Optimization**: By spreading sales over multiple years, Michael managed his income levels to stay within lower tax brackets.
- **Deferred Income**: Reduced immediate tax burden by deferring some income to future years.

Overall Impact

By strategically implementing these legal loopholes, Michael effectively optimized his tax outcomes. Here's a summary of his tax savings and strategies:

- **Roth IRA**: Provided tax-free growth and withdrawals, allowing long-term tax benefits.
- **Specific Identification Method**: Reduced taxable gains on Bitcoin and optimized gains on Ethereum.
- **Crypto Loans**: Deferred capital gains and maintained portfolio exposure.
- **Income Deferral**: Managed taxable income across multiple years to benefit from lower tax brackets.

Detailed Example Calculations

1. **Specific Identification Method for Bitcoin**:

- Purchased 1 BTC at $600 in 2016, another 1 BTC at $1,000 in 2017, and another 1 BTC at $5,000 in 2018.
- Sold 1 BTC in 2023 for $50,000.
- Selected the BTC purchased at $5,000 to minimize gains.
- Taxable Gain: $50,000 (sale price) - $5,000 (cost basis) = $45,000 (taxable gain).

1. **Income Deferral**:

- Sold 2 BTC and 25 ETH in December 2023, generating substantial gains.
- Planned additional sales in January 2024, deferring the income to the next tax year.
- Managed income to stay within the 15% long-term capital

gains tax bracket for 2023 and 2024.

Conclusion

Michael's case demonstrates the effective use of various legal strategies to optimize cryptocurrency tax outcomes. By utilizing tax-advantaged accounts, specific identification methods, crypto loans, and income deferral, Michael successfully minimized his tax liabilities while staying compliant with tax regulations. This proactive approach allowed him to manage his investments strategically and achieve significant tax savings.

Case Study 3: The Dangers of Using Illegal Loopholes in Cryptocurrency Taxation

Background

David is a 45-year-old freelance web developer who began investing in cryptocurrencies in 2015. By 2022, his portfolio had grown significantly, and he was looking for ways to reduce his tax liability. Instead of consulting a tax professional, David decided to use various illegal loopholes to evade taxes, believing that the decentralized nature of cryptocurrencies would protect him from detection.

Situation Analysis

David's portfolio included:

- **Bitcoin**: Purchased 10 BTC in 2015 for $300 each.
- **Ethereum**: Purchased 100 ETH in 2016 for $10 each.
- **Various Altcoins**: Investments in multiple altcoins, with both gains and losses.
- **Stablecoins**: Held USDC for liquidity purposes.

In 2022, David decided to sell a significant portion of his holdings to take advantage of the market boom. However, instead of reporting these transactions, he attempted to use several illegal loopholes to avoid paying taxes.

Illegal Loopholes Used

1. **Failing to Report Cryptocurrency Transactions**
2. **Using Offshore Accounts to Hide Assets**
3. **False Reporting of Transactions**
4. **Using Anonymity to Evade Taxes**

Strategy 1: Failing to Report Cryptocurrency Transactions

Implementation: David believed that because cryptocurrencies are decentralized, he could sell his holdings without reporting them to the IRS.

Action:

- Sold 5 BTC for $250,000.
- Sold 50 ETH for $175,000.
- Did not report these transactions on his tax return.

Result:

- **Immediate Consequence**: David avoided paying taxes on $425,000 in gains initially.

Strategy 2: Using Offshore Accounts to Hide Assets

Implementation: David transferred a portion of his cryptocurrency to an offshore account in a country with lenient tax laws, believing this would hide his assets from the IRS.

Action:

- Transferred 3 BTC and 30 ETH to an offshore account.
- Used the offshore account for additional trading.

Result:

- **Immediate Consequence**: David thought he was evading detection and avoiding taxes on these assets.

Strategy 3: False Reporting of Transactions

Implementation: David submitted false information on his tax return to minimize his taxable income.
Action:

- Claimed inflated cost bases for the cryptocurrencies he did report, significantly reducing the reported gains.
- Reported losses from altcoins he never sold to offset gains.

Result:

- **Immediate Consequence**: Reduced his reported taxable gains, further minimizing his tax liability.

Strategy 4: Using Anonymity to Evade Taxes

Implementation: David used privacy coins and decentralized exchanges that do not require identity verification to conduct transactions anonymously.
Action:

- Converted some of his holdings into privacy coins like Mon-

ero (XMR) and used decentralized exchanges for trading.
- Believed that these actions would prevent tax authorities from tracking his transactions.

Result:

- **Immediate Consequence**: Continued to trade and profit from these activities without reporting them, avoiding immediate tax obligations.

Consequences of Illegal Loopholes

In 2023, the IRS began to use advanced blockchain analytics tools to track cryptocurrency transactions and identify potential tax evasion. David's activities raised red flags, and the IRS initiated an audit of his tax returns.

Audit and Investigation

1. **Discovery**:

- The IRS discovered unreported sales of BTC and ETH amounting to $425,000 in gains.
- Identified the transfer of assets to offshore accounts and trading activities not reported.
- Detected discrepancies and false reporting on his tax returns.

1. **Penalties and Fines**:

- **Unreported Transactions**: Fined for failing to report $425,000 in gains.

- **Offshore Accounts**: Faced penalties under the Foreign Account Tax Compliance Act (FATCA) for not reporting foreign financial assets.
- **False Reporting**: Fined for submitting false information on tax returns, including penalties for fraud.

1. **Legal Action**:

- The IRS referred the case to the Department of Justice for criminal prosecution.
- David was charged with tax evasion, fraud, and failure to report foreign accounts.

Financial Impact

1. **Back Taxes**: Required to pay back taxes on the $425,000 in unreported gains.
2. **Penalties and Interest**: Assessed penalties and interest on unpaid taxes, significantly increasing his financial liability.
3. **Legal Fees**: Incurred substantial legal fees to defend himself against the charges.

Criminal Charges and Sentencing

1. **Criminal Charges**: Convicted of tax evasion, fraud, and failure to report foreign accounts.
2. **Sentencing**: Sentenced to 18 months in federal prison and fined $250,000 in addition to the back taxes, penalties, and interest owed.

Summary

David's case demonstrates the severe consequences of using illegal loopholes to evade cryptocurrency taxes. While he initially avoided paying taxes, the eventual audit and investigation led to significant financial and legal repercussions, including hefty fines, penalties, and imprisonment. This case highlights the importance of staying compliant with tax regulations and seeking professional advice to manage tax obligations legally and ethically. Engaging in illegal tax evasion strategies not only risks severe financial penalties but can also result in criminal charges and damage to one's personal and professional reputation.

Case Study: Comparing Tax Implications of Holding vs. Frequent Trading

Emma and John both started investing in cryptocurrencies in January 2020 with an initial investment of $50,000. They adopted different investment strategies:

- **Emma**: A long-term holder, she planned to hold her investments for at least three years.
- **John**: A frequent trader, he actively traded his holdings to capitalize on market fluctuations.

By December 2022, we will compare their portfolios' performance and the tax implications of their strategies.

Initial Investment Details

- **Emma's Portfolio**:
- 2 Bitcoin (BTC) at $25,000 each.
- **John's Portfolio**:
- 2 Bitcoin (BTC) at $25,000 each.

Emma's Long-Term Holding Strategy

Emma held her 2 BTC without any transactions until December 2022. The value of Bitcoin appreciated as follows:

- **January 2020**: 1 BTC = $25,000
- **December 2022**: 1 BTC = $50,000

Emma's Portfolio in December 2022:

- 2 BTC worth $100,000

Tax Implications for Emma

1. **Holding Period**: 3 years (long-term)
2. **Cost Basis**: $50,000
3. **Fair Market Value in December 2022**: $100,000
4. **Unrealized Gain**: $100,000 - $50,000 = $50,000

If Emma decides to sell in December 2022:

- **Long-Term Capital Gains Tax Rate** (assuming 15% for her income bracket):
- Capital Gains = $50,000
- Tax Liability = $50,000 * 15% = $7,500

John's Frequent Trading Strategy

John actively traded his 2 BTC, making several trades throughout the three years. Here's a simplified version of his trading activity:

1. **First Trade** (June 2020):

- Sold 1 BTC at $30,000
- Purchased 1.2 BTC at $25,000 each

2. **Second Trade** (December 2020):

- Sold 1.2 BTC at $35,000 each
- Purchased 1.5 BTC at $28,000 each

3. **Third Trade** (June 2021):

- Sold 1.5 BTC at $40,000 each
- Purchased 2 BTC at $35,000 each

4. **Fourth Trade** (December 2021):

- Sold 2 BTC at $45,000 each
- Purchased 2.5 BTC at $38,000 each

5. **Final Position** (December 2022):

- Sold 2.5 BTC at $50,000 each

John's Portfolio in December 2022:

- Total sales proceeds: $325,000
- Total cost basis: $262,000 (cumulative purchases)
- Total gains: $325,000 - $262,000 = $63,000

Tax Implications for John

1. **Holding Period**: Multiple short-term transactions
2. **Short-Term Capital Gains Tax Rate** (assuming 35% for his income bracket):

Tax Calculation for Each Year:

- **2020**:
- First Trade:
- Gain: ($30,000 - $25,000) = $5,000
- Tax: $5,000 * 35% = $1,750
- Second Trade:
- Gain: (1.2 BTC * $35,000) - (1.2 BTC * $25,000) = $12,000
- Tax: $12,000 * 35% = $4,200
- Total 2020 Tax: $1,750 + $4,200 = $5,950
- **2021**:
- Third Trade:
- Gain: (1.5 BTC * $40,000) - (1.5 BTC * $28,000) = $18,000
- Tax: $18,000 * 35% = $6,300
- Fourth Trade:
- Gain: (2 BTC * $45,000) - (2 BTC * $35,000) = $20,000
- Tax: $20,000 * 35% = $7,000
- Total 2021 Tax: $6,300 + $7,000 = $13,300
- **2022**:
- Final Sale:
- Gain: (2.5 BTC * $50,000) - (2.5 BTC * $38,000) = $30,000
- Tax: $30,000 * 35% = $10,500

Total Tax Liability for John:

- 2020: $5,950
- 2021: $13,300

- 2022: $10,500
- **Total Taxes Paid**: $29,750

Comparison of Outcomes

Emma (Long-Term Holder):

- Total Portfolio Value in December 2022: $100,000
- Tax Liability if Sold in December 2022: $7,500
- **Net Value After Tax**: $100,000 - $7,500 = $92,500

John (Frequent Trader):

- Total Portfolio Value in December 2022: $125,000 (including final sale proceeds)
- Total Taxes Paid Over 3 Years: $29,750
- **Net Value After Tax**: $125,000 - $29,750 = $95,250

Summary

- **Emma's Strategy** (Long-Term Holding): Resulted in a lower tax liability due to the long-term capital gains tax rate and less frequent trading.
- **John's Strategy** (Frequent Trading): Despite achieving higher gross gains, John faced a significantly higher tax liability due to the short-term capital gains tax rate applied to his frequent transactions.

Conclusion

This case study demonstrates the different tax implications of long-term holding versus frequent trading of cryptocurrencies. While frequent trading can potentially lead to higher gross gains, the short-term capital gains tax rate can significantly reduce the net gains compared to long-term holding, which benefits from a lower tax rate. Investors should carefully consider their trading strategies and the associated tax implications to optimize their net returns.

Tips for Building a Portfolio to Maximize Profits

Creating a statistically sound portfolio to maximize profits involves blending quantitative analysis with sound investment principles. Here are some tips and tactics to help you build a robust portfolio:

1. **Diversification**

- **Asset Allocation**: Diversify across different asset classes (cryptocurrencies, stocks, bonds, etc.) to reduce risk. Allocate a portion of your portfolio to each asset class based on your risk tolerance.
- **Cryptocurrency Diversification**: Within the cryptocurrency space, diversify among different types of cryptocurrencies (e.g., Bitcoin, Ethereum, altcoins) to avoid overexposure to any single asset.

2. **Risk Management**

- **Volatility Assessment**: Use historical data to assess the volatility of each cryptocurrency. Higher volatility can mean higher risk, but also higher potential returns.
- **Position Sizing**: Determine the size of each position based

on its risk level. A common rule is not to allocate more than 5-10% of your portfolio to a single high-risk asset.

3. Modern Portfolio Theory (MPT)

- **Mean-Variance Optimization**: Utilize MPT to construct a portfolio that offers the maximum expected return for a given level of risk. This involves calculating the expected return and standard deviation (risk) of each asset, as well as the correlations between them.
- **Efficient Frontier**: Aim to create a portfolio that lies on the efficient frontier, where you achieve the highest possible return for a given level of risk.

4. Rebalancing

- **Regular Rebalancing**: Periodically rebalance your portfolio to maintain your desired asset allocation. This helps lock in gains and reduce exposure to overperforming assets that may be overvalued.
- **Threshold Rebalancing**: Rebalance whenever an asset class exceeds a predefined threshold (e.g., 5% deviation from target allocation).

5. Quantitative Analysis

- **Backtesting**: Test your investment strategies using historical data to assess their performance. This can help identify the most effective strategies for different market conditions.
- **Factor Analysis**: Identify and invest in factors that have historically outperformed the market, such as momentum,

value, and low volatility.

6. Tax Efficiency

- **Tax-Loss Harvesting**: Offset gains with losses by selling underperforming assets at a loss to reduce your taxable income.
- **Long-Term Holding**: Benefit from lower long-term capital gains tax rates by holding investments for more than one year.

7. Market Timing

- **Dollar-Cost Averaging (DCA)**: Invest a fixed amount regularly, regardless of market conditions. This reduces the risk of making large investments at unfavorable times.
- **Technical Analysis**: Use technical indicators (e.g., moving averages, RSI) to identify entry and exit points. However, be cautious as this approach can be speculative.

8. Research and Due Diligence

- **Fundamental Analysis**: Evaluate the underlying value and potential of each cryptocurrency. Consider factors such as technology, team, market demand, and competitive landscape.
- **Stay Informed**: Keep up with market news, regulatory developments, and technological advancements to make informed investment decisions.

9. Advanced Tactics

- **Staking and Yield Farming**: Earn passive income by staking cryptocurrencies or participating in yield farming. This can provide additional returns beyond price appreciation.
- **Arbitrage**: Exploit price differences between different exchanges or markets. This requires quick execution and a thorough understanding of market mechanics.

Example Portfolio Construction

Let's construct an example portfolio using some of these principles:

Step 1: Asset Allocation

- **Cryptocurrencies**: 50%
- Bitcoin (BTC): 20%
- Ethereum (ETH): 15%
- Altcoins (e.g., Cardano, Polkadot, Solana): 15%
- **Stocks**: 30%
- Technology Sector: 10%
- S&P 500 Index Fund: 10%
- Emerging Markets: 10%
- **Bonds**: 10%
- Government Bonds: 5%
- Corporate Bonds: 5%
- **Cash/Cash Equivalents**: 10%

Step 2: Risk Management

- **Volatility Assessment**: Choose cryptocurrencies with a mix of high and low volatility to balance risk.
- **Position Sizing**: Limit high-risk altcoin positions to 5%

each.

Step 3: Modern Portfolio Theory

- **Mean-Variance Optimization**: Use software tools to optimize the portfolio based on historical return and risk data.
- **Efficient Frontier**: Ensure the portfolio lies on the efficient frontier.

Step 4: Rebalancing

- **Regular Rebalancing**: Rebalance quarterly to maintain target allocation.
- **Threshold Rebalancing**: Rebalance if any asset class deviates by more than 5% from its target.

Step 5: Quantitative Analysis

- **Backtesting**: Backtest the portfolio using historical data to ensure it meets your performance and risk criteria.
- **Factor Analysis**: Include assets that exhibit strong momentum and value characteristics.

Step 6: Tax Efficiency

- **Tax-Loss Harvesting**: Sell underperforming assets to offset gains.
- **Long-Term Holding**: Hold a portion of cryptocurrencies for more than one year.

Step 7: Market Timing

- **Dollar-Cost Averaging (DCA)**: Invest a fixed amount monthly.
- **Technical Analysis**: Use moving averages to identify optimal entry points.

Step 8: Research and Due Diligence

- **Fundamental Analysis**: Regularly review the fundamentals of each cryptocurrency.
- **Stay Informed**: Subscribe to market news and updates.

Step 9: Advanced Tactics

- **Staking and Yield Farming**: Stake a portion of Ethereum for additional returns.
- **Arbitrage**: Monitor exchanges for arbitrage opportunities.

Conclusion

Building a statistically sound portfolio involves a mix of diversification, risk management, quantitative analysis, and informed decision-making. By following these tips and tactics, you can create a robust portfolio designed to maximize profits while managing risk effectively. Always remember to stay informed and adapt your strategy based on changing market conditions and personal financial goals.

No-Fuss Way to Track Crypto Taxes for the Lazy Trader

Managing cryptocurrency taxes can seem daunting, especially for those who trade frequently or are not detail-oriented. However, with the right tools and strategies, you can simplify the process and stay compliant with minimal effort. This chapter will guide you through a straightforward approach to tracking your crypto taxes efficiently, even if you consider yourself a "lazy trader."

1. **Automate Everything**

Use Cryptocurrency Tax Software

There are several cryptocurrency tax software options designed to make tax tracking and reporting as easy as possible. These tools connect directly to your exchanges and wallets, automatically importing and categorizing transactions. Popular choices include:

- **CoinTracking**
- **CryptoTrader.Tax**
- **Koinly**
- **TokenTax**
- **ZenLedger**

Benefits of Tax Software

- **Automated Data Import**: Connect your exchange accounts and wallets to import transaction data automatically.
- **Tax Calculations**: Automatically calculate capital gains, losses, and taxable income.
- **Reports Generation**: Generate tax reports, including Form 8949, Schedule D, and other relevant forms, ready for filing.

2. Use a Single Exchange When Possible

Consolidate your trading activities on one or two exchanges to minimize the complexity of tracking multiple accounts. This reduces the number of places you need to import data from and simplifies your overall tax reporting.

3. Set Up Alerts and Reminders

Use calendar alerts or app notifications to remind you of important tax deadlines and regular maintenance tasks, such as:

- **Quarterly Reviews**: Review your trades every three months to ensure all data is correctly imported and categorized.
- **Tax Deadlines**: Set reminders for key tax dates, such as estimated tax payment deadlines and annual tax filing deadlines.

4. Simplify Your Trading Strategy

Adopt a trading strategy that minimizes the number of taxable events. Consider these approaches:

- **HODLing**: Holding your assets for the long term can reduce the frequency of taxable events and benefit from lower long-

term capital gains tax rates.
- **Set It and Forget It**: Use automated trading strategies or bots that execute predefined trades without requiring constant manual intervention.

5. Use a Separate Wallet for Each Tax Year

Create a new wallet for each tax year to easily segregate your transactions by year. This makes it simpler to track and report your activities accurately without mixing up transactions from different tax periods.

6. Track Your Cost Basis Efficiently

Understanding your cost basis is crucial for calculating capital gains and losses. Use the following methods to keep it simple:

- **First-In-First-Out (FIFO)**: This is the default method where the first coins you bought are assumed to be the first ones you sold.
- **Specific Identification**: If your tax software supports it, you can specify which coins you sold, which can help optimize your tax outcome.

7. Automate Backups

Regularly back up your transaction data to prevent loss of records. Set up automated backups through your tax software or use cloud storage solutions to keep your data safe.

8. Professional Help for Complex Situations

If your trading activity is complex or if you're unsure about specific tax implications, consider consulting with a tax professional who specializes in cryptocurrency. They can help you navigate tricky situations and ensure you remain compliant with tax laws.

9. **Keep Up with Tax Regulations**

Tax regulations for cryptocurrencies are continually evolving. Stay informed by subscribing to newsletters, following relevant social media accounts, or using resources provided by your tax software. This ensures you're aware of any changes that might affect your tax obligations.

Practical Steps for the Lazy Trader

Step 1: Choose a Tax Software

Select a cryptocurrency tax software that suits your needs and create an account. Most software offers a free tier or trial period.

Step 2: Connect Your Accounts

Link all your exchanges and wallets to the tax software. Ensure it supports all platforms you use.

Step 3: Import Transactions

Allow the software to import your transaction history. This process might take some time, depending on the number of transactions.

Step 4: Review and Categorize

Periodically review imported transactions for accuracy. Correct any discrepancies and categorize transactions as necessary (e.g., staking rewards, mining income).

Step 5: Generate Reports

At the end of the tax year or quarterly, use the software to generate the required tax reports. Ensure all data is accurate and complete.

Step 6: File Your Taxes

Use the generated reports to file your taxes. You can do this yourself using tax software like TurboTax or hand over the reports to your tax professional.

Tools and Resources

Recommended Tax Software

- **CoinTracking**: Comprehensive tracking with advanced analytics.
- **CryptoTrader.Tax**: User-friendly interface with accurate tax calculations.
- **Koinly**: Supports multiple countries with detailed reporting.
- **TokenTax**: Direct integration with TurboTax.
- **ZenLedger**: Focus on ease of use and quick setup.

Additional Resources

- **IRS Cryptocurrency Tax Guidelines**: Stay updated with the latest tax regulations.
- **Cryptocurrency Tax Calculators**: Online tools for quick calculations.
- **Cryptocurrency Tax Forums**: Communities like Reddit for peer support and advice.

By following these no-fuss strategies and leveraging the right tools, even the laziest traders can manage their cryptocurrency taxes efficiently and stay compliant with minimal effort.

Conclusion: Simplifying Your Crypto Tax Journey

Navigating the complexities of cryptocurrency taxation can seem overwhelming at first, but with the right tools, knowledge, and strategies, it becomes manageable and straightforward. Throughout this book, we've explored the foundational concepts of crypto taxation, detailed filing instructions, strategies for minimizing tax liability, international considerations, and legal insights.

We've equipped you with practical tools and resources to streamline your tax reporting process, ensuring you stay compliant while maximizing your investment potential. From automating your tax tracking to understanding the nuances of legal loopholes, you now have a comprehensive guide to confidently manage your crypto taxes.

Remember, the key to simplifying your crypto tax journey lies in staying organized, leveraging technology, and keeping abreast of regulatory changes. Whether you are a seasoned investor or just starting, these insights will help you navigate the tax landscape with ease.

As you embark on your cryptocurrency trading journey, armed with this knowledge, we wish you the best of luck. May your investments flourish, your trades be profitable, and your tax season be stress-free. Happy trading!

Good luck, and may your crypto ventures bring you prosperity and success!

I've done the research, so you don't have to! If you found this book helpful and would like to support my work, consider buying me a coffee (or latte). Your support not only means a lot but also helps me continue creating valuable content to make your crypto journey easier. You can show your appreciation at ko-fi.com/yaaylatte. Thank you and may the profits be with you!

www.ingramcontent.com/pod-product-compliance
Lightning Source LLC
Chambersburg PA
CBHW070318230526
45470CB00002B/929